CLASSROO

By Rob Salter

Cartoons:
Phil Hailstone

Published by:

Teachers' Pocketbooks
Laurel House, Station Approach,
Alresford, Hampshire SO24 9JH, UK
Tel: +44 (0)1962 735573
Fax: +44 (0)1962 733637
Email: sales@teacherspocketbooks.co.uk
Website: www.teacherspocketbooks.co.uk

*Teachers' Pocketbooks is an imprint of
Management Pocketbooks Ltd.*

Series editor – Linda Edge

© Rob Salter 2016

This edition published 2016
ISBN 978 1 906610 85 2

E-book ISBN 978 1 908284 62 4

British Library Cataloguing-in-Publication Data
– A catalogue record for this book is available
from the British Library.

Design, artwork and graphics by Efex Ltd.
Printed in UK.

Contents

The presence problem

We all know teachers who command attention the moment they walk into a room; they have immediate presence that communicates itself to pupils, often without a word having been spoken.

But pupils don't sit in class thinking: *'I respect this teacher; they have great presence'*. It's an unconscious process. Children and teenagers 'read' their teachers and respond on an emotional level, depending on what they look and sound like; what kind of example they set and how they carry themselves.

It can be hard to get useful feedback from lesson observations about the kind of impact you make on your class. Occasionally, teachers may get the comment that they 'lack presence' in the classroom. This is a euphemism for 'poor behaviour management' and is rarely accompanied by any ideas about how to increase that elusive presence.

Your classes, however, are full of children who have no such inhibitions concerning feedback and who will, if you learn to look for and interpret it, provide you with limitless feedback about your level of presence in the classroom – every hour of every day!

Presence is taught in other contexts

As teachers we are used both to reflecting on unconscious or sub-conscious processes and to teaching about them. We do it when we show pupils how to infer or how to analyse the subtext in a novel or play, for instance. Yet, when it comes to teacher training and development, learning about and exploiting this level of communication barely features.

Business people, politicians and actors – all professionals who need to command an audience – are routinely trained in how to increase their presence and become more effective and compelling communicators. So why not teachers?

Competence in this area is a key indicator in how effectively we manage our classes and provide quality teaching over the span of a career.

Linking acting and teaching

It was when working with PGCE students who were struggling to assert themselves in the classroom that I first saw how useful they would find the acting techniques I was teaching my 'A' Level Drama students.

Later in my career I became a teaching and learning coach and over the years developed the eclectic approach to establishing effective classroom presence that I will be outlining in this book. I now regularly work with teachers to:

- Interpret feedback that students are giving them
- Understand the subtext and implications of their reactions to events in class
- Maximise the power of body and voice
- Understand how to use space in the classroom effectively
- Show how assertiveness, rapport and status can be a transformational triad
- Conquer their demons, eg if you struggle to say 'no' in life, you may well struggle in the classroom

Presence and persona

The first key to understanding is this:

> **Presence is the effect created by your teacher persona**

So, what is a teacher persona and how do you create one?

There are various ways to think about this question, but the most fun is to go and see some stand-up comedy. In most theatre performances, the actors have to ignore the audience to draw them into the world of the play. Comedians, on the other hand have, to work *with* their audience, whose response is crucial to the entertainment. They have to engage with and control hecklers and they have to make the audience like them; otherwise, they get no laughs and die the death of a thousand cuts. Not that different from the classroom…

From stage to classroom

Of course, there are differences between a stand-up comic's job and a teacher's, but the similarities are clear. Any good stand up will have a likeable persona but will also be sufficiently dominant and assertive not to be victimised by their audience or by hecklers. Remember how, apparently effortlessly, your favourite teachers managed to inspire, entertain and control you? It's the same thing.

On walking into their classrooms, many successful teachers seem to put on an old, familiar coat – their teaching persona. The minute they enter the room their voice, tone, posture and attitude transform. This professional persona is not 'who they are'; it is 'who they are in the classroom', a construct that helps them to do their job.

New teachers, especially, baulk at the idea that they cannot 'be themselves' in front of a class. Only after bitter experience, do they start to 'wear the coat' (or suit of armour in some cases!) that helps them to survive. One of the things you'll learn from this Pocketbook is a set of complementary skills to help you create a winning persona.

Surely you need more than just presence?

All good teachers are willing and able to use school discipline systems when necessary, it's just that the best ones rarely seem to need to. They have managed to transcend the need for sanctions in all but the most difficult situations.

In fact, all teachers, with enough awareness and practice, can reach that level of competence and influence, developing a truly powerful presence in the classroom.

Working nowadays with teachers at various stages of their careers, I teach **a triad of skills** which, combined, create this powerful presence and allow you as a teacher to back up your persona with confidence, based on the ability to be **assertive**, to create **rapport** and to understand how to switch **status** at will.

As well as the skill triad, other areas I'll be covering in this book include ways to build relationships and to connect with your students using techniques from NLP, psychology and acting.

Skills triad

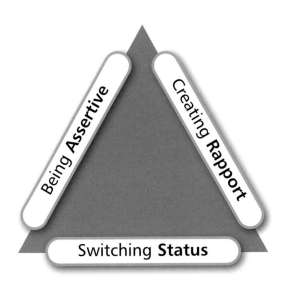

Reading it vs doing it

'*I hear and I forget. I see and I remember. I do and I understand.*' **Confucius**

As a good teacher, you will have internalised the old adage above. Therefore, when you plan a lesson, you will be looking for opportunities for your pupils to 'show they know' and to apply the information they have learnt.

So with this book. My training as an actor and then as a Drama teacher taught me to find ingenious ways of physicalising learning for my students. Unfortunately, you are not with me in my Drama studio, or opposite me in a coaching session, so I have to trust that you will be inspired enough by the content to try out some of the ideas for yourself.

Even if all you do is to stand in front of your class, keeping your head still and notice the effect on your pupils and on yourself, you will have refunded yourself the cost of this book, because just that one device, used regularly, can have a huge effect on how you are perceived by any audience.

Once you begin to understand the principle that small changes can have a huge impact on your teaching, I hope you'll be inspired to apply more of the ideas described here.

Status

Improvisation and the teacher

Most of the ideas in this section of the book have been developed from Keith Johnstone's work on 'status' in his influential book *Impro**. Johnstone's ideas on improvisation and storytelling gave birth to Theatresports (competitive improvisation on stage) and eventually to the hit TV show *Whose Line is it Anyway?* They have also been applied to sales training and his book is required reading in some businesses, because of its insights into creativity and team-working. It can also be used very successfully to help teachers understand behaviour management.

In some cases, an understanding of status transactions alone has helped teachers transform the way in which their pupils perceive and respond to them. By learning to raise their status in the eyes of their pupils, often by using very simple tricks or devices, they have been able to get their classes, groups and individual students to listen to them and take them seriously.

If, let's say, a tiny change in how you move can affect others' perception of your power and importance in any given situation significantly, surely it is worth exploring?

**Impro – Improvisation and the Theatre* by Keith Johnstone. Bloomsbury 1981

What do we mean by status?

Essentially, Johnstone made his discoveries about status when working with actors on how to make their improvisations seem less contrived and more 'normal'. When he instructed pairs of actors to *'try to get their status just a little above or a little below'* their partner's, their work was transformed. What they said, how they said it, how they moved, behaved and looked, all changed to accommodate the status they were playing.

What they tapped into is the fact that in all social interactions there is a hierarchy, and nothing is accidental or 'motiveless'. Participants may choose to be more dominant or less authoritative (high status or low status); they may try to maintain or alter their own status in the group or to raise or lower that of others, but *every inflection and movement implies a status*.

Sample script

In the sample script below B has been waiting for A, who is late.

A: *Hallo*
B: *Hallo*
A: *Been waiting long?*
B: *Ages*

Johnstone uses this short exchange to get actors to consider different ways of shifting A's and B's relative status.

The usual first interpretation is that A is apologetic then embarrassed, while B is irritated and unforgiving. B plays high status and lowers A's status. However, it's possible to run the conversation with both A and B playing high status (A is nonchalant in the face of B's response) or both playing low status (B smiles at A's arrival and makes a joke of 'ages' by exaggerating how he/ she says it then laughing.)

The effects are completely different.

More about status

Additionally, it became clear to Johnstone that we all have a 'preferred status' that we're not necessarily aware of until it is pointed out. It is independent of social or professional standing. As Johnstone explains: *'Status is a confusing term unless it's understood as something one does. You may be low in social status but play high – and vice versa'*. He rejects the more loaded terms 'dominant' and 'submissive' concluding that status is a useful term as long as you know *'the difference between the status you are and the status you play'*.

Once Johnstone and his actors understood all this, they started thinking not just about *what* was being said, but *why* it had been said. My approach to teacher training is to help teachers not only become aware of their own preferred status but of the subtext and implications of their everyday classroom interactions.

High and low status teachers

Meet Jean and Jane. They have been teaching for the same number of years and produce diametrically opposite reactions in their pupils.

Jean

Erm...stop! That's enough!

Voice:	high pitch
Breathing:	shallow, throat
Movement:	jerky, fidgeting
Emotions:	angry, red face
Appearance:	messy
Position:	all over the room

We could call Jean a compulsive low status player. By compulsive, I mean that she may not realise that her behaviour is low status as a teacher but everything about her non-verbal cues, her appearance and her voice screams: *'Abuse me!'*

High and low status teachers

Jane

Jane, on the other hand, has her classes eating out of her hand. Like Jean, she is not consciously playing a status but is a compulsive high status player. Everything about her appearance and reactions communicates: *'Respect me!'* And her pupils do.

> Good morning everyone...

Voice: slow and low
Breathing: from stomach
Movement: still, centred

Emotions: calm in control
Appearance: smart
Position: front, centre

Of course Jean and Jane are extreme examples. Most teachers have aspects of both or are more like one or the other, depending on which class is in front of them.

The important question is: if you feel like Jean, can you become more like Jane? The answer is, of course!

This book will provide clear advice on how you can use your voice, breath, movement and appearance to create a high status teaching persona that will work for rather than against you.

Instant high status – the head still trick

If you are struggling to see what I mean about raising and lowering status, try this little exercise with someone you know well:

1. Have a conversation with them about anything you like.
2. Tell them you've been asked to try an experiment at work. They have to look at you and try to identify any changes in you and in the way that you are coming across.
3. Carry on the conversation but keep your head perfectly still.
4. Ask them if they detect any difference; the majority of people will tell you that they feel a difference but will struggle to define it.
5. When you ask if they think that you have become more or less authoritative, they will always say more authoritative.
6. Then start touching your face and perhaps adding some short 'erms' into your speech and ask again.
7. You will find that their perception of you has changed and your status has dropped.

Particularly if you try the head still trick standing up, you may well notice a change in your breathing and voice tone. You tend to go slower and lower. We'll return to voice projection later on but for now, it is worth noting how your breathing tends to change and become deeper.

Reading classroom interactions

The following noisy class scenario will be familiar. The two teacher responses are low and high status respectively.

Pupil

Teacher A

Teacher B

	Pupil	**Teacher A**	**Teacher B**
Says	Oi! Shut up you lot!	Yes, can you quieten down everyone?	Don't shout, Stevie. I don't need you to do my job for me. OK everyone, eyes on me and silence in 3, 2, 1......
Means	*You aren't doing your job so I'll do it for you.*	*He's right, you know. I really am not doing my job effectively.*	*I'm on to you; don't publicly try to lower my status while pretending to raise it. Now watch me do my job.*
Implication	*I control this room; not you.*	*Please feel free to subtly point out my inadequacies whenever you feel like it...I won't realise you're doing it.*	*I'm in charge. You'll need to do better than that to catch me out.*

Common status lowering situations

What emerges from the above scenario is that young people are often masters of subtext and therefore you need to be too. Some pupils spend all day long trying to irritate their teachers, whilst not getting into trouble. In order to counter their efforts, you need at least to understand the subtext and implications of your responses to standard classroom events. Some educational theorists call this *'with-it-ness'* or *'the art of running a classroom while having eyes in the back of your head'* and are clear that it's a vital skill for an effective classroom practitioner.

It can even make sense to rehearse some potential scenarios in your head, if they happen on a regular basis, to make sure that you are being congruent in your responses. Think:

1. How is this pupil trying to lower my status?
2. How can I raise it?

Raising your status under pressure

1. Late Arrival

Arriving late to a lesson can be interpreted as a way of trying to lower the teacher's status. The subtext is: *'Your lesson is not important enough to be on time for'*, with a possible side dish of *'My late entrance is going to be much more exciting than your lesson'*.

When dealing with it, be sure to lower the status of the latecomer in some way. (It goes without saying that humiliating them, sarcastic comments or other negative/aggressive responses are not acceptable.) Some teachers will temporarily deny latecomers entry, choosing to keep them outside for a moment and depriving them of an audience for their excuses. They then ensure that any latecomer catches up quickly with missed work. In lowering their status, you raise your own.

Raising your status under pressure

2. Mysterious noises

I always liken these to a Mexican standoff. The subtext is: *'I am going to enjoy watching you try to work out who this is and deal with it effectively'* and of course the scary implication is: if you can't, then that's an open invitation to anyone else to join in.

Keeping your status high in a tense situation where pupils are obviously trying to lower it can be very challenging. Especially because they are trying to lure you in by encouraging you to accuse someone who can then deny any responsibility. Avoid this trap by calmly speaking to the whole class, minimising the importance of the noises:

'OK. Very funny. Obviously we have some comedians in here. The noises need to stop'.

It may seem counter intuitive, but you need to say this without anger or any sense that you are particularly riled. This kind of challenge is designed to lower your status by making you reactive, so your next move should be high status and proactive, designed to divert the class's attention from the 'spectacle'. You could break the impasse by improvising a group activity which involves moving places or changing partners, remaining aware of who the culprits might be and separating them out. Think about other ways of effecting a diversion by changing the mood or activity and have some tactics up your sleeve.

Reading the 'script' of your lessons

Low and high status reactions

	John	Jamie	Teacher A	Teacher B
Says	Sir/ Miss… Jamie took my pen!	I haven't got it!	Give it back Jamie	Boys, don't waste my time. Now, which one of you is moving? You need to decide quickly.
Means	*I can interrupt you whenever I want. You are not important enough for me to raise my hand.*	*Of course I haven't; I gave it to Frank, sitting behind me, when John wasn't looking.*	*Please?*	*Yes, I have noted that you interrupted me and I'm not happy about it. No I am not going to accuse Jamie so that he can plead innocence. Who took it is of no consequence.*
Implication	*This interruption is more interesting than your lesson.*	*Hopefully I can distract you into this entertaining sideshow.*	*Yes, I've bought into this sideshow and now I'm trapped. Now you can plead innocence and I can get angry.*	*However, there is an immediate consequence to your misbehaviour but I am not going to decide who moves; that will just get me drawn into the argument over who has the pen. In the lag time that I have given you, the pen will re-appear anyway and I can decide if I want to actually move one of you or not.*

Reading the script of your lessons

The point about interactions such as these is that they happen in a split second and there can be many of them in one lesson. Once you have trained yourself to note the subtext, you will realise that there is rarely ever one correct response, as long as the response that you do make addresses both the subtext and the implications.

For example, in the above scenario, whether you actually separate John and Jamie depends on many things:

- Lesson context – perhaps the pace or activity needs changing as pupils are losing focus in general?
- Your relationship with these two boys – what are the chances of a secondary conflict developing with one of the boys who has to move?
- How quickly the pen 'returns' and whether you would rather give a warning and then monitor their behaviour

Micro-moves – the politics of eye contact

Most of us pay no attention to how much eye contact we make with others. It has a lot to do with which status we feel most comfortable playing in life. In the classroom, however, being aware of the effects of eye contact is vital.

Coming up are two contrasting examples of how to use eye contact in a high status way.

In the first, maintain eye contact for a couple of exchanges, long enough to make your point; in the second, break eye contact early.

Maintain eye contact to raise your status

In the example above, the subtext is: *'I expect you to comply. There's nothing further to discuss.'*

Breaking eye contact too early could send a message to the pupils that you do not really stand by your warning. Keeping eye contact strongly suggests that you do.

Break eye contact to raise your status

Your response to requests for bathroom breaks may well be dictated by school policy. Occasionally children will really need to go but more often than not, their request is actually just to determine whether or not you will let them out of the classroom. The problem with saying 'yes' is that in some ways you have lowered your status and become 'the teacher who will let us out of the room', thereafter prompting many other such requests.

In this example, the teacher breaks eye contact quickly and in a very high status way. The subtext is: *'I am not even considering it. I've dismissed it because we both know you are 'trying it on'.* In this situation, maintaining eye contact would simply be an invitation to open a discussion or to argue and so to lower your status.

Be a status expert

1. Remember that you manage behaviour from the moment your pupils first see you. However much you are rushing, always attend to the way you greet your class. Make sure that it is in a high status way: stand in the doorway or face the line of pupils, totally still and speak in a low, calm voice (whatever the pupils are doing). When you set the tone in this way, your calmness and authority will communicate itself to the pupils and their behaviour will improve.

2. Learn to play both high and low status and to switch between the two. Keith Johnstone's idea about teaching is that great teachers are status masters: *'All those jokes on teacher are to make him drop in status.'* Status masters change their status first, before the pupils can do it for them. Learn, for example, to share a joke with the class but then become very still and impose quiet before moving on.

3. Know when and why to play both high and low status. For example, you may be playing low status with one pupil by crouching down to work at their level and speaking quietly and then getting up quickly to play high status with a pupil who is off focus across the room. Showing your awareness of who needs what and what is happening around you marks you out as a teacher who is in control.

High and low status behaviours

Low Status	The Implication	High Status	The Implication
Arrive late and flustered	*I can't manage my time*	Arrive early and greet pupils at the door	*I am organised and in control*
Allow pupils to enter the class at will	*This is your space, come in when you like*	Insist on a line up outside/ pupils behind chairs	*This is my space and I decide when and how you enter*
Never insist on silence	*You decide on the noise levels*	Insist on silence at the start of the lesson (register/ silent starter)	*I can create silence at will*
Be constantly moving, and responding to requests	*I'm uptight and not calm*	Power pose (see next two pages) and use stillness regularly (during silent activities)	*I'm the adult in control here. I'm calm so you can be too*
React immediately to misbehaviour	*I am highly reactive and you can have fun winding me up*	Be calm under pressure and take time to proactively decide the best course of action	*No point trying to wind me up; it won't work*

The science of status

Social psychologist Amy Cuddy's TED Talk on the science of 'faking it till you make it' is highly recommended as a contribution to understanding how to develop confidence and presence. You'll find it via your search engine. It's called 'Your body language shapes who you are?

Can you fake it till you make it? Can you 'power pose' for just a little while and actually experience a behavioural outcome that makes you seem more powerful?

TED TALKS
Amy Cuddy

Do our non-verbals govern our feelings about ourselves?

2 Mins

Power pose:

Submissive pose:

Is it true that our bodies change our minds?

The power pose

In her talk, Cuddy describes the result of an experiment that she carried out at UC Berkley, which compared the blood results of volunteers who had held either a 'power pose' or a 'submissive pose' for two minutes. As the graphic shows, the volunteers who held the power pose all created significant hormonal changes in their blood chemistry within a very short space of time.

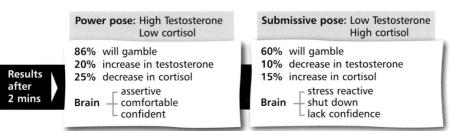

Results after 2 mins

Power pose: High Testosterone Low cortisol	**Submissive pose:** Low Testosterone High cortisol
86% will gamble	**60%** will gamble
20% increase in testosterone	**10%** decrease in testosterone
25% decrease in cortisol	**15%** increase in cortisol
Brain ⎰ assertive / comfortable / confident	**Brain** ⎰ stress reactive / shut down / lack confidence

She also tells the story of a student whose journey from fear to confidence mirrored her own and reinforced in her the following realisation: *'She had actually faked it until she had become it. So she had changed. And what I want to say to you is, don't fake it till you make it, fake it till you become it.'*

Can playing high status win you an election?

You could cite many reasons for the relatively inexperienced Senator Barack Obama beating his more experienced rival John McCain to the US Presidency in 2008. One is that Obama was either coached, or was naturally able, to look and sound presidential by appearing high status, while his opponent unconsciously played classic low status.

For an example of high and low status players on the same platform, check out the online footage from the 2008 US Presidential TV Debates.

Head still

Smile

Voice: slow & low

Back straight

Arms relaxed

Blinks too much

Frown

Voice: high pitched

Hunched

Arms tense

Jerky hand movements

Assertiveness

'Inside-out' rather than 'outside-in'

'Working out what my rights were in the classroom and learning to protect them, was the single biggest factor in improving my behaviour management.'
Julie, Science teacher

This was Julie's feedback following coaching on how to play high status. She was enjoying the changes she saw in both her pupils and colleagues from something as simple as keeping her head still when she spoke, for example. However, status, in many respects, is an 'outside-in' approach. As the saying goes: *'You can fool some of the people some of the time; but you can't fool all of the people all of the time'*.

It was time to try an 'inside-out' approach to complement the performance skills that Julie was now using to create her persona, which is why we moved on to discuss assertiveness.

The assertiveness triangle

Creating an impression of authority is important in building a teaching persona that pupils will respond to but if your persona lacks 'teeth' you are likely to get found out and suffer as a result.

There are three positions on the 'Assertiveness Triangle':

Aggressive people are often dominant or bullying personalities, (they can be found in the classroom and the staffroom alike). They jealously guard their own rights, and are unconcerned with the rights of others.

Passive people can be seen to agree with the bullies and are often 'victim types'.

Assertive personalities protect their own rights, and the rights of others.

Whilst the above is obviously a gross simplification, it is a useful guide. (I've found it a helpful model for teaching pupils in the context of bullying awareness).

Where are you on the triangle?

The next stage is to locate yourself on the triangle and to do so you will need to understand the concept of rights for you as a private person and then as a teacher.

- If, for example, you find yourself reacting defensively to relatively minor misdemeanours, or if you often find yourself in confrontation with pupils, you may have aggressive tendencies and may need to focus more on respecting others' rights as well as your own

- If you are easily intimidated by people who appear more 'powerful' or 'knowledgeable' than yourself, you may be subtly giving away your right to be treated with respect

- If, however, you are, or decide to become, someone who neither looks up to nor down on others, then you will feel entitled to protect that right if someone criticises or otherwise demeans you

A teacher's rights

When I first started teaching I was a fairly passive individual with little idea of my rights as a teacher in the classroom. I gave most of them away without realising what I was doing. Below are some rights you can reasonably claim – and what happens when you give them away compared to when you protect them.

I have the right to...	When I give my rights away I...	When I protect my rights I...
Silence when I speak	Talk over your noise	Insist on silence/ wait for it/ use a silent starter
Criticise	Ignore misbehaviour	Correct/ offer constructive, critical feedback
Impose sanctions	Do not create consequences for misdemeanours	May choose to set detentions
Choose what we do in lessons	Allow myself to be swayed over choice of activities	Decide what needs to be done and do it
Set high standards	Accept whatever you give me	Require you to repeat sub-standard work
Eject a student from my lesson	Allow you to stay in class against my better judgment	Send you out temporarily/ permanently
Decide where you sit	Let you sit with friends, regardless of what is best for a particular lesson or situation	Insist on a seating plan if that is appropriate

The skills of assertiveness

Once you have decided to both claim and protect your rights in the classroom, you will need to develop and practise some basic skills. They may seem odd at first but as with any new skill, they simply require practice.

The skills in question, involve learning to say 'no' and how to give and receive criticism assertively. They are vital skills to master in class, as in life.

In my case, it was only really after having learned and applied them in my teaching that I could also use them in my personal life. In this way, my teaching experience allowed me to grow as a person in my own right.

As you will see, I discuss saying 'no' in the context of your professional relationships as well as with pupils.

The theory of 'no'

It's a small word but one which I struggled with for years until I learned the following two helpful techniques:

A Get the word out early and do not apologise for it. Sometimes it helps to say the word and simply look away (playing high status).

B Where a pupil persists, employ the 'broken record technique'. In essence, 'broken record' involves repeating what you want (or don't want) up to three times, without raising the tone of your voice, becoming angry, irritated, or involved in side issues. Continually repeating a request or a refusal will ensure the discussion does not become side-tracked by irrelevant argument. The key is to stay calm, be very clear in what you want, stick to the point and not give up.

If you try this, you will find that three really is the 'magic number'; very few people ask four times for anything.

'No' and 'broken record' in class

Here's a selection of possible uses of the 'broken record technique' in classroom situations.

1

Pupil: *'Sir, can I sit next to Sanjeet?'*

You: 'Stay where you are.'
Pupil: 'But why?'

You: 'Stay where you are.'
Pupil: 'But Sir I can't concentrate here.'

You: 'You are doing fine, stay where you are.'

2

You: *'Jasmina, I'd like you to move next to Mae.'*

Pupil: 'But why Sir?'
You: 'Jasmina, you need to move next to Mae.'

Pupil: 'Sir, if you let me stay here I will work.'
You: 'Jasmina, you need to move.'

Pupil: 'But Sir!'
You: 'You need to move, thanks, Jasmina.'

3

Pupil: *'Sir can we do X instead of this?'*

You: 'No, you need to finish this.'
Pupil: 'Why?'

You: 'You need to finish it.'
Pupil: 'But it's boring.'

You: 'You need to finish it and then we will move on to something different.'

Saying 'no' in the staff room

Standing firm and saying no is a vital skill in adult professional life. As a coach, I meet many teachers who report that senior colleagues assume they will say yes to almost any request. These teachers worry about offending others or seeming unco-operative if they refuse. The following are two examples of how to choose an assertive response as a professional.

THE REQUEST	WHAT YOU REALLY FEEL	YOUR FEARS	ASSERTIVE RESPONSE
'Can we switch rooms?' (Last minute request from a colleague)	It will unsettle the class/ I'll have to change my lesson plan	I don't want to seem unco-operative/ you are senior to me/ what if I need your help in future?	*'It's going to really mess up my lesson, so no. Next time, if you give me warning, it will be easier.'*
'Can you get this work to me by tomorrow?' (Last minute request for a large report)	I will be up till 2am doing this! Why tell me now?	Someone must be leaning on you to get this done. You might get into trouble if I don't	*'I'm happy to do it but no, I cannot guarantee by tomorrow. I'll need more time.'*

Giving criticism

Like many other aspects of assertiveness, giving criticism does not always come naturally, especially if you are the kind of person who tends to avoid conflict at all costs. However, once you learn the 'rules' of managing criticism, you'll become more comfortable with it:

- **Think win/win**. You ultimately want a certain behaviour to stop. It makes sense to focus solely on the behaviour and to try to get agreement that it will stop, rather than becoming personal or using phrases such as *'you always ...'* or *'you never...'*

- **Use I rather than *you* statements**. Aim to get them to take responsibility and to focus on your feeling of disappointment. It's harder to argue with your feelings than to react negatively to a *'you did this or that' statement. 'I was very happy with your work until just then...'* is a good choice

- **In or out?** Ask yourself if you can correct the pupil in front of the class without creating too much resistance or whether it would be better to send them outside to speak to them. After sending a pupil out, play high status. Leave them for at least a minute before you go out and ask: *'Why did I send you out?'* Then leave a long pause, forcing them to take responsibility for their actions

Receiving criticism

All of us at some point in our careers will face open criticism from a pupil or pupils during a lesson. Students may try to lower your status publicly and you need to be prepared to deal with them in a way that leaves your teaching persona intact:

- **Don't get angry**. Becoming angry will play into the hands of the heckler, whose aim is to derail your lesson and throw you off course

- **Acknowledge the grain of truth**. If a child tells you that they are bored or that the work is boring, for example, there is no reason not to acknowledge what they are feeling. *'Well, I'm sorry you feel that way,'* delivered in a deadpan manner will work well, particularly if it is followed by the high status comment, *'but this is the work that we need to do now, so we need to get on with it.'* Remember, as the teacher you have the right to decide on the work set

- **Do not accept insults**. You have the right to be treated respectfully. This right applies in all areas of your life. Certain children will be rude to you, simply because they wish to challenge and undermine your authority. A simple answer such as: *'No, I'm not going to let you be rude to me'* and a possible warning about sanctions will normally suffice

The 'niceness' problem

'At one point I stood in front of them and forcefully said 'I am your teacher!' As I said it, something clicked in my mind: I realised that perhaps I hadn't been acting that way.' **Angie, Maths Teacher**

One of the reasons I began writing about learning to teach was that I recognised the process as a 'learning journey' and that often the things that I struggled with in the classroom were the things that I also struggled with in life.

One of those things was a lack of reference experiences for being assertive enough to 'lead' or 'manage' a group of adolescents. I remember clearly the first lesson I ever taught in school and how odd it seemed to be 'on the other side' of the desk. I had done well at school and had learned to get on in life by being pleasant and polite to people. What I didn't realise was that this would only work in the classroom if I first learned to be respected as a leader.

Dealing with diffidence

The Craft of the Classroom by Michael Marland is a UK classic of classroom management, written by a serving headteacher in the 1970's. The book, though dated in some respects, remains popular because of Marland's wisdom and his ability to get to the nub of the 'teaching problem'.

> *'There is amongst many young teachers, a diffidence that makes them pull back from imposing their will: the result, too often is that a clique of pupils in the class imposes its will instead. This is resented by the other pupils and the resentment sours those pupils' relationships with the teacher..... There is also a very understandable fear which many teachers have of losing the affection or good relationship of the pupils...there is nothing so pathetic as the sight of a desperately anxious teacher casting away more and more of his standards as frantic sops to rapid popularity.'*

For Marland, then, diffidence – appearing reserved and lacking in confidence – is a key problem.

The passive/ aggressive mindset

A teacher who has fallen into the trap that Marland describes will end up giving away their rights as teacher in the hope of winning popularity. They will struggle to say 'no' or to criticise poor behaviour and will be forced into playing low status to the higher status of the clique of more assertive pupils who will be allowed to dominate.

Instead of being assertive, they are in danger of becoming passive aggressive. This happens when negative emotions and feelings build up and are then held in on either:

- A self-imposed need for acceptance by another/ others
- Dependence on others or to avoid even further arguments or conflict

You may recognise some of the classic passive aggressive behaviours listed on the next page. They all involve a reluctance or refusal to deal effectively with the problem at hand and they rarely lead to a resolution. Similar problems will keep occurring until the passive aggressive individual is ready to act assertively.

Passive aggressive behaviours

Passive Aggressive Behaviour	Explanation
Non-communication	There is clearly something to discuss but you don't raise it, eg letting poor behaviour go unchecked.
Avoiding/ignoring	You are so angry you feel you cannot speak calmly, eg not expressing your legitimate displeasure at poor behaviour.
Evading problems and issues	Burying your head in the sand: *'Let's just get through this lesson'*.
Self-pity	The 'poor me' scenario.
Blaming	Blaming the poor behaviour solely on the pupils.

After a while, people who have been bottling up their feelings tend to express their anger in destructive and exaggerated ways. In short, they may well move straight from passive to aggressive behaviour and explode with anger.

We all know how destructive this can be for classroom relationships. Students tend to see explosions of anger as a sign of low status in their teacher – and, often, a source of entertainment. This can lead to more goading in the hope of a further reaction.

Dealing with your own anger

The kind of teacher that Marland describes struggles to express anger at all, even when they are entitled to feel angry and to express that they have been made to feel angry by the poor behaviour of their students.

What they quickly learn is that *children with too few boundaries go in search of them*; that their pupils actually want them to 'be the teacher' and to set and enforce clear, consistent parameters and rules. They are simply pushing to see how far they can go and what they can get away with.

We all have to learn to accept our own anger, take responsibility for it and learn to express it in an acceptable and constructive way, whilst working hard to manage the poor behaviour which may have caused it assertively and proactively.

Acting angry

The best teachers agree that once they learn to be assertive they also learn the proper context for expressing anger at appropriate moments. Crucially, they learn to channel their own anger when an incident of serious misbehaviour occurs and to leave a 'thinking gap' which allows them to express that anger in a way which remains high status and assertive without being either passive aggressive or explosively aggressive.

Obviously this is an art which cannot be mastered overnight. Here are a few pointers for what to do in the heat of the moment:

1. Take your time to decide on a course of action.
2. Stand 'on stage' for maximum presence.
3. Breathe: produce your most resonant voice, speak slower and lower than normal.
4. Allow the anger to show in your voice but do not shout.
5. Give an instruction, eg to move a student or remove them from the room altogether.

Practice makes perfect and perfect is an effective response which does not lead to unwanted 'secondary behaviours' (such as a pupil arguing with or shouting at you).

Moving forward

Focusing on and practising the skills on the previous page will help you to create a high status persona backed up by assertive action.

Once you **acknowledge** and begin to **protect your rights**, learn to **say 'no'** and **give and receive criticism** effectively, you will begin to see others' reactions to you change significantly.

However, a really skilled teacher is a master of human interaction. Rather than hiding behind their persona, they inhabit it, learning over time to connect with groups and individuals on a deep level and managing to develop their influencing skills.

These teachers learn to teach with a powerful classroom presence, based ultimately on the quality of their relationships. This takes us to the third element of the skills triad: rapport.

Rapport

The third ingredient

'*You know, kids don't learn from people they don't like.*' **Rita Pierson (TED Talk)**

As explained earlier, I teach a triad of skills that need to be balanced and used together for maximum effectiveness. So far we have looked at how status and assertiveness interact. The final ingredient is rapport.

To work successfully with your pupils over the course of an academic year, you will need to learn to create rapport. When we look in a moment at the concept of 'pacing and leading', it will become clear that it is vital to have created rapport with someone before you can lead them to do what you need them to do.

Rapport is a naturally occurring phenomenon, but it's within the context of Neuro Linguistic Programming, or NLP, that it has been studied and from which we can draw helpful pointers for classroom presence. (As an approach to effective communication and how to influence others, NLP also gives us the concepts of framing, calibration, sensory acuity and behavioural flexibility. These are useful tools for developing impact and presence and, by extension, for managing our most challenging classes. More about these concepts later in the book.)

NLP in a nutshell

Developed in the 1970's by American academics, Richard Bandler and John Grinder, NLP is defined as an approach to communication, personal development and psychotherapy. Bandler and Grinder set out to model excellence in communication and to devise a series of principles which could be taught and replicated in other contexts. The excellent communicators they chose to model were the most competent and experienced therapists of the day, people who could create remarkable change in their patients, often by first creating rapport on a deep level.

NLP works on a number of presuppositions:

- **We are always communicating** – even with our body language and tonality
- We need to **respect another person's model of the world** if we wish to influence them
- **The meaning of the communication is the response you get** – ie what you intended may not have been communicated. Accept that interpretations can differ
- **If what you are doing isn't working, do something else** – behavioural flexibility is key
- **There is no failure, only feedback** – do not blame yourself, just develop the sensory acuity to recognise what is and is not working

Defining rapport – mirroring

The most effective way to understand a concept is often through your own experience of it. I have often noticed, for example, that when talking with a friend with whom I feel comfortable and 'in sync', we tend subconsciously to mirror each other's body language.

Bandler and Grinder noticed this phenomenon in the therapists they observed who were able to create excellent trust and relationships with their clients. They concluded that matching and mirroring a person's body language is part of the way we create rapport.

Defining rapport – pacing and leading

I'm not advocating that you start mirroring your pupils to get them to like you! That would create a whole set of problems for you.

What I am suggesting is that you bring an understanding of mirroring into one of the key applications of rapport: the idea of 'pacing and leading'. This concept pre-supposes that in order to influence a pupil, or anyone else, without creating resistance, you need to pace (ie create rapport with them) before you can lead them to change their behaviour.

The ratio of pacing to leading that seems to work is 3:1. See it as a series of dance steps: 'pace, pace, pace, lead'.

Strictly Pacing and Leading

And one...and two ...and three...

But sir! I'll miss my bus.

Pacing and leading

Imagine walking into a clothes shop one day, unsure of what to purchase but wanting to browse. Then imagine two different shop assistants. One comes up to you straight away and points out the items on sale, asking what you are interested in buying. The other, greets you and lets you browse for a while before asking if you need any help. Which do you prefer?

With few exceptions, people tend to prefer the second shop assistant, finding the first one 'pushy'. The second allows you to get comfortable before approaching you about a possible purchase.

The first shop assistant is not 'pacing before they lead'. They're making the same mistake as teachers who are less successful in persuading pupils to do things they may be ambivalent about (ie work!).

Pacing and leading in action

Imagine a student with her head on her desk:

- The pushy teacher calls over to her and gives an instruction
- The teacher who paces first, walks over to the student's desk, crouches down and mirrors her body language and breathing rate, before asking if she understands the work. Only then does the teacher guide the pupil to carry on

Which teacher is likely to experience most success?

When you have established rapport, so much more is possible in your lessons. The next three pages give examples.

Teaching all your pupils

Teachers with a good understanding of rapport will be more likely to pace the learning ability of each pupil in their class before they try to lead them to their educational objectives. Knowing who can and cannot do what in your class is vital.

Working as a Special Education teacher, I used to see teachers use the same lesson plan for all of their classes in a year group, regardless of the ability of the class. Their idea of 'scaffolding learning' and 'differentiation' was to speak slower to the lower ability classes. Thankfully, these days such teachers are rare!

Research has shown that most teachers, after having asked a question wait just one second for a student to answer! Do you at least give pupils thinking time after asking a question? Do you only take answers from those wildly gesticulating in your direction? Or do you differentiate your questions according to who you would like to answer? Or ask people to answer based on a random name generator or by drawing lots?

Differentiation within the lesson and scaffolding in your planning both demonstrate to your pupils that you can **empathise with them** as learners.

Listening

Really good teaching is like a satisfying conversation. Two people listen to each other and create synergy together; that is they create something new, something that didn't exist before and that couldn't exist without both participants' inputs. That is why the same lesson can and should be different with different classes; not just because you may have differentiated in the planning but because the response that you get to the material will never be the same twice.

For this to happen we have to learn to listen to and value what our pupils give us in class, and create opportunities for them to offer feedback and ideas during the lesson.

- Ask open questions and reflect back answers to pupils. Simply repeating an answer to show that you have absorbed the contribution can make a student feel valued
- Encourage creativity through role plays, script / story writing, group presentations
- Plan group and class discussion
- Allow peer teaching and learning
- Listen for signs of distress or misunderstanding and find ways to deal with these

Let your students know that **you value their input**.

Pupil distress

It's so easy when faced with a pupil with challenging behaviour to go through the motions of the discipline system without ever finding the cause of the behaviour. Understanding the nature of a student's difficulties can help a teacher to formulate a personalised strategy for creating a good working relationship. This idea is explored in the film *Freedom Writers*, the story of Erin Gruwell – a teacher at Woodrow Wilson High School in Long Beach California.

The film is based on a simple premise: some children are too distressed to learn. Gruwell recognised that the chaotic lives of her pupils were preventing them from accessing their education. She saw that before she could lead them to education, she had to pace their current situations and listen to what was troubling them. She came up with the idea of giving them journals in which they were encouraged to write about their lives. Their journals (not marked and not part of the syllabus) allowed the students to express themselves, to feel heard for the first time and to trust their teacher.

Building rapport is essential to classroom presence; it is fundamental in developing positive relationships with your students. Later, we'll see what else NLP can teach us about building relationships but first, a look at how, by harnessing positive energy, you can make your presence felt.

Three Circles of Energy

Defining presence

> *'People will forget what you said, people will forget what you did, but people will never forget how you made them feel'* **Maya Angelou**

Over and over, when people are asked to recall their memories of favourite teachers from the past, they speak about teachers who:

- Interacted regularly with pupils, often outside of class
- Knew pupils well and related to them as individuals
- Had high expectations of them and brought out their potential
- Had a passion for their subject and an ability to communicate that passion
- Created a classroom climate in which they felt 'safe', motivated and valued

Whenever I am asked to observe or assess a new teacher, I find that I am looking for the x-factor in their lessons. Are pupils connecting to the learning? Do they feel excited and passionate about what they are doing? Is there a 'buzz' in the room? Do they enjoy being in this lesson with this teacher? While it might seem as if the elusive quality some teachers have is something magical that you cannot control, in reality, it's something that can and should be learned.

Defining the x-factor

It's no coincidence that these days the term 'x-factor' brings to mind a popular TV talent show. There's a strong connection between a powerful presence on stage and one in the classroom. I mentioned stand-up comedians at the start of this book, but it was only when I came across the work of acting coach and former teacher Patsy Rodenburg that I realised how much talented actors and singers also depend on their presence to communicate.

If you watch TV talent shows, you'll find they often focus on 'the moment' – the sudden realisation by judges and audience that the tiny figure in the distance on stage is managing to 'reach' the back of the auditorium in some way. There is a connection.

In her book *Presence*, Patsy Rodenburg defines this phenomenon. Just like a talent show judge, she – as a voice coach for the Royal National Theatre in London – would sit in the auditorium and listen to auditions where it became apparent that some actors had 'it', while others had 'it' fleetingly, or didn't have 'it' at all.

After literally thousands of auditions, Rodenburg finally defined 'it'. Star performers tap into what she describes as a shared energy with their audience. Rodenburg calls this **second circle energy**.

First circle energy

To understand second circle energy, we need to know a bit about first and third circle energy, as conceived and described by Rodenburg.

Rodenburg describes first circle energy as 'energy that falls back into you'. It's the 'circle of self and withdrawal'.

I am in **first circle** when I am self-conscious or nervous, or when I am at the centre of my own small circle of energy which I am unable or unwilling to share. If I am alone, then being in first circle is not a problem for me. If I am in class or on stage however, then I may seem distant or – worse – dull, as my energy is focused inwards. I may well lose my audience.

Teachers at the start of their careers who are self-conscious and unconfident about being 'on stage' and wonder 'how am I doing?' are trapped in first circle. They struggle to make an impact, tending to drain or sap their classes' energy rather than spark or invigorate it.

First circle energy

Third circle energy

At the other end of the scale is third circle energy.

A performer in **third circle** certainly attracts attention, but they may seem 'showy', 'false' or 'trying too hard'. They push energy outwards; they may puff out their chest and their voice may be loud but they are not able or willing to share their energy authentically with those around them. They are in some way trying to control others' response and in so doing, are sending out diffuse energy beyond the energy field of the recipients.

Third circle energy can be useful and desirable, for instance where feigned charm is required. Say your job is greeting customers in an airport: it's impossible to be completely genuine with every one of the hundreds of customers you meet in a day, but as a professional you need to appear smiling and helpful. You need to seem lively and in control, and you need people to do what you tell them. With third circle energy you can engage superficially and gain compliance and co-operation.

Third circle energy

Third circle energy

Third circle energy sounds initially attractive, and indeed there are times when teachers might need to be in third circle, eg:

- Telling a year group off
- Controlling a corridor or dining room
- Dealing with difficult pupils you do not know on the playground
- Injecting energy or 'rallying the troops'
- Mounting a one-off charm offensive with an angry parent

In third circle you can protect yourself. People tend to withdraw from you, so you can deflect unwanted intrusions and this too can be useful in teaching.

However, adopting a third circle teaching persona as a default is destructive and negative. Rodenburg calls third circle energy 'the circle of bluff and force'. As such, it leads in the classroom to aggression, sarcasm, insensitivity and arrogance. You never genuinely interact with your students; you dominate, lack awareness of others, shout a lot and become overbearing. Your students soon see that you're not really interested in them. Good teachers with real presence know that the energy of 'bluff and force' has little place in the classroom.

Second circle energy

'Great teachers teach in second circle.' **Patsy Rodenburg**

Second circle is a shared circle of energy, described by Rodenburg as **the energy of connecting**.

In **second circle** the teacher or performer delivers their message powerfully to their audience, but it's not a one-way street. Energy is received back from the audience – there's both give and take – a real connection. This is the x-factor that we call 'talent' in performers who are able to draw you into the inner world of their thoughts and feelings and take you on a 'journey' with them that changes you in some way. A singer or actor makes us feel the emotions in the play or song. A great teacher who connects with and is passionate about their material, enables their pupils to do the same.

One way to understand this is to think back to your own teachers and recall those who had this effect on you or who you felt had 'presence'. You were never bored: their lessons probably felt intimate, inclusive and often 'special' and you may remember feeling present and alive yourself.

Second circle energy

In the video http://youtu.be/Ub27yeXKUTY of Rodenburg lecturing actors in New York City, she clearly describes the movement between the three circles as they relate to performance. Her view is that it's only in second circle that we are really present with our audience and only then can we really connect with them.

Moving between the circles

Rodenburg developed her ideas as a result of her frustration with the 'myth' of talent, as she saw it. For her, the magical x-factor had to be defined, so that it could be properly taught. Not to teach it or explain its workings amounted to a form of cruelty.

So how can you learn about and tap into second circle energy? A good way to start is to look for examples of second circle communication around you and to watch for people moving in and out of the three circles of energy.

One of the best examples online is an improvisation class run by Hollywood actor Alan Alda, at The Centre for Communicating Science at Stonybrook State University of New York. Alda's class is called *Improvisation for Scientists* and includes footage of Science PhD students learning how to use acting and improvisation skills to 'get them out of their heads' when talking about science.

The before and after videos are very instructive. We see highly intelligent people trying to perform in first circle with no connection to the audience. Alda makes them personalise their message and insists that they be free, present and in a shared circle of energy before they try again. The results are striking: http://www.centerforcommunicatingscience.org/improvisation-for-scientists/

Your second circle checklist

Patsy Rodenburg's checklist for second circle and recognising when it occurs will now make good sense. Awareness is the key!

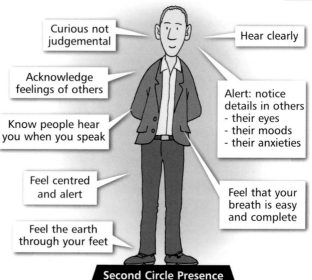

Curious not judgemental

Hear clearly

Acknowledge feelings of others

Alert: notice details in others
- their eyes
- their moods
- their anxieties

Know people hear you when you speak

Feel centred and alert

Feel that your breath is easy and complete

Feel the earth through your feet

Second Circle Presence

What does second circle feel like?

It's one thing to grasp the theory of cultivating second circle presence and another to experience it. Here's a coaching conversation I had with a Science teacher who had just had a breakthrough in terms of understanding presence.

'I am starting to feel relaxed in my own classroom and as a result I feel like I can see what the kids are actually doing, almost for the first time. That applies to those who are not working or misbehaving. Before, I only found out if they weren't working when I got their books in to mark. Now I'm moving around and marking as I go. I'm also not so reactive to their behaviour [**third circle**]. I can see what they have done and can decide on the appropriate sanction, or more likely remind them, with a warning, of how actions have consequences. One of the best parts is that I am no longer worried about my ability to teach and influence them [**first circle**]. I just do it and I feel like I am properly in the room with them [**second circle**].'

The 'I' perspective

Now let's examine second circle in more detail and uncover some of the ingredients that make it work:

1. Storytelling – when you speak about yourself, people get a sense that they know you. This may seem like an obvious comment but it's something powerful that teachers can tap into for leverage with their classes. For instance, I will often try to find a true story from my experience to illustrate a point. My favourite teacher at school used this technique for teaching English literature. She would find an example from her own life that made the texts seem more relevant to us. It helped create a bond between her and us.

2. Class Discussion – I was surprised when I did a mini survey in school and found that this was the most popular activity in my own classes. I would re-arrange the desks into a long rectangle, seat students around the outside and ask them for true stories related to the topic that we were covering. Their experience was validated as everyone listened to each other's contributions in silence. In a round table discussion on bullying, one pupil, a shy and withdrawn boy, listening to his peers speaking freely and being heard, found the confidence to admit that he had been a victim of bullying. He then participated very constructively in the discussion about strategies to combat bullying in class.

What's in it for me?

Cultivating second circle energy involves making sure that your class buy into your lessons. In marketing, a key question is *'What are the needs of the customers?'* and, ultimately, what will persuade them to buy a particular product. Your pupils are asking themselves and answering this question every lesson. They are looking to understand WIIFM – what's in it for me?

Lots in it for me		Nothing in it for me
'They make it fun'	>	'It's so boring'
'We always learn a lot'	>	'We don't learn anything'
'I didn't think I would be interested but I am'	>	'I hate this subject'
'My teacher likes me'	>	'My teacher hates me'
'They make us work'	>	'They can't control us'
'I've got better at it'	>	'I'm terrible at it'

As teachers, we are constantly being reminded about showing progress and engagement through data but we're not often asked about our students' own 'assessment criteria' for our lessons. Taking note of your students' criteria will give you vital feedback as to whether you are a teacher with presence.

Passion for your subject

Are you passionate about your subject? Luckily, most teachers are, although this is not necessarily the same as being passionate about teaching it to 30 disruptive 12 year-olds on a Wednesday afternoon!

> *I recently observed a Maths teacher start a lesson with a group who obviously didn't inspire him and with whom he had made little attempt to create rapport. 'Books open,' he drawled. 'We're doing decimals'. About half the class had opened their books, but without checking to see who was engaged, operating steadfastly in first circle, he turned his back to the class and wrote on the board for around five minutes. Needless to say, he spent the next five minutes in third circle trying to manage the behaviour of a group of disaffected pupils.*

It's impossible to maintain a passion for your subject in all circumstances but it is possible to fake passion on occasion! Why bother? Because if you don't, you become jaded very quickly and disappear into first circle, as in the example above. You will then veer between first and third circles and lose out on the opportunity to share energy with your classes.

Passion – what's in it for you?

If you recognise yourself in the Maths teacher on the previous page, you can train yourself to become a more effective communicator by practising being in second circle in front of a class. You may find that, having lost your passion, you re-discover it in helping pupils connect with powerful ideas and concepts.

Surely a fairly important 'What's in it for me?' for you as a teacher is to enjoy lessons, getting the most out of your job.

A passion for teaching

The fact that you are reading this book demonstrates a passion for teaching and for refining and improving your professional skills. To develop your skill in communicating in the classroom:

- Spend time studying communication. NLP for example or voice production
- Consider coaching: does your school run a coaching programme? If not, consider virtual coaching (for details of my own virtual coaching programme, see page 126)
- Take a look at the *Effective Classroom Communication Pocketbook*
- Thousands of websites deal with educational content. TED is a great place to start

Try these three TED talks to begin with:

1 Rita Pearson, *Every Kid Needs a Champion*
(on being a teacher that kids remember) http://youtu.be/SFnMTHhKdkw.

2 Sir Ken Robinson, *Do Schools Kill Creativity?*
(one of the most watched Ted talks) http://youtu.be/iG9CE55wbtY

3 Sugata Mitra, *Learning on the Edge of Chaos*
(how children teach themselves and others) http://youtu.be/dk60sYrU2RU.

Only Connect

The sharpest tools in the box

It should be clear by now that teachers with great classroom presence have a high degree of self-awareness and a fairly sophisticated understanding of human interactions and relationships. Being able to read subtle signals and respond in finely-judged and nuanced ways is part of what it takes to be a highly effective teacher. Some teachers seem to have this kind of knowledge and ability intuitively; most of us, though, need input and practice to get there.

This section looks at a range of NLP and other techniques you can use to help establish and develop your classroom presence.

Develop your sensory acuity

We are always communicating. Even when we're not speaking, we're transmitting messages – and so are our students. Developing your sensory acuity means learning to observe the external clues received from other people and using them to interpret what people are thinking and feeling. The teacher who notices the non-verbal cues that show whether a student really understands a question, or who 'reads' that two particular pupils sitting together are likely to distract each other during the lesson, is decoding body language to anticipate problems before they occur.

Without thinking about it much, you are probably already sensitive to changes in behaviour and motivation caused by environmental factors:

- Time of day
- Weather
- Previous lesson
- Whether certain influential students are present or not
- Conflicts that students may bring in from previous lessons
- How engaged the class may be in the work

A teacher who is 'with-it', who has 'eyes in the back of their head', will not get caught out by missing these subtle signals.

Behavioural flexibility

However, simply being aware of the more subtle signals that your students are giving you is just the first step. The next is being flexible enough to alter what you are doing and to respond to how successful the new course of action has been, being prepared to try something else if necessary.

Being adaptable in this way is key to creating a powerful teaching persona. Many teachers fail to respond quickly enough to the changing feedback, or lack the confidence to think of alternative choices 'on their feet'. Sticking doggedly to a plan that is clearly not working undermines your reputation and professionalism. Be bold and pro-active:

If your class has been working quietly for just ten of the 30 minutes you need them to allocate to the task and you pick up increasing signs of them losing concentration, what could you do to refocus their attention?

When this happened in a Year 9 English lesson, the teacher called a five-minute break from the activity. She asked two pupils to read out their two best consecutive sentences and asked other class members to comment on why those sentences worked well. She then refocused the class on the work. The short break and the extra input changed the unsettled mood, provided guidance and made getting down to intense concentration easier.

Framing and reframing

The NLP concept of 'framing' can be applied usefully to the classroom and is helpful in developing a powerful teacher persona. Framing refers to the way we put things in contexts and how these contexts provide meanings. By altering the frame we can alter the meaning. The concept is simple enough to understand. Imagine you come home after a terrible day at work and talk your day over with your partner:

Everything went wrong; your classes were all horrendous and you are exhausted. Your partner reminds you that you did not get to bed until late the previous night and that you had a difficult journey to work. Perhaps you were just tired and stressed?

Your frame had been profoundly negative and you had seen yourself as the victim. Your partner, however, made you see the day through an alternative frame. Perhaps because you were not at your best you did not react to events as you usually would and your classes picked up on that?

Having reframed the day you now have an opportunity to get a good night's sleep and put things right tomorrow.

The next day reframed

Imagine now going to school the next day and transforming your experience and that of your classes. You are rested and positive and have the skills and energy to create lessons and manage classes so that you create a positive learning frame in every lesson. The things that the pupils were saying and doing yesterday have not changed significantly but your response to them has.

From this relatively common experience, we can conclude that:

- You create your own experience
- It is often your mood that is responsible for the mood and behaviour of your pupils
- You can take responsibility for your moods and thus influence theirs
- You are responsible for creating a positive learning frame
- You can choose how you behave often in spite of how you feel

Cultural architects

I am a fan of team sports, particularly football, and I've borrowed the following ideas from sports psychology.

The class described above could be compared to a successful football team, where each player is 'buying into' and executing the 'frame' of their coach. Any successful football team will have what are called 'cultural architects'. These are often the most senior players, the ones with most experience and social sway in the team, and the ones who are able to communicate the vision of the coach, even when he or she is on the sidelines.

Football coaches may use up to three cultural architects in a team – in attack, midfield and defence – to ensure that the team plays within the agreed frame.

The important difference between a sports coach and a classroom teacher is, of course, that the coach gets to pick their team and appoint their own cultural architects. As a teacher you may well have cultural architects in your classes, but these influential pupils often have a frame that is very different from yours, and one which they can use to lead the whole class away from work!

Reframing cultural architects

> *'Teaching is a reasonably long-term activity and the relationships that succeed will be built up by a long-term policy. The relationships at which you should be aiming are those achieved by, say, the end of the year, not the end of the first week.'* **Michael Marland**

The mark of an experienced teacher with great presence, is that they know exactly how to handle their most challenging pupils and 'get them onside'.

An inexperienced teacher will often feel at the mercy of these pupils and be unable to impose their frame on the class. The powerful 'clique' that Marland describes earlier (pages 47-8) may well impose its will instead. The key skills for re-framing are:

- Be proactive, not reactive. Remember, 'status masters' change their status first, before their students can do it for them
- Develop a high degree of behavioural flexibility and be able to balance both high and low status, assertiveness and rapport as necessary
- Think long term. Relationships with some individuals can be seen as a 'journey towards respect' and can take the best part of an academic year to get right. Don't give up!

The balancing act

Three important factors to bear in mind about building relationships with cultural architects:

1. Most pupils, and especially the 'difficult' ones, are far more likely to accept authority or discipline from you if they feel that they already have a relationship with you.
2. You need to be able to create a positive relationship, often against the will of a pupil, who may not initially want it.
3. If you fail to observe the pacing and leading rule (pace three times before you lead), you are likely to create more resistance than if you had observed the rule.

Often pupils such as these are highly sensitive to the way in which different teachers approach them and will ultimately appreciate the efforts of a teacher who is obviously doing what they can to involve them in the learning and make them feel as though their influence is being both acknowledged and channelled positively.

Rapport bombing

One teacher told me how he'd learnt the value of 'rapport bombing' his cultural architects.
His tactics included:

- Greeting them at the start of the lesson
- Not isolating them at the back of the room
- Giving them positive attention
- Using their name
- Catching them being good and publicly praising them
- Communicating high expectations for them

Getting it right – the seating plan

Exercising your right to decide on where pupils sit in your room, can give you tremendous leverage in managing both friendship groups and individuals.

There will be times when you want students to work in friendship groups and times when you don't. Whether creating random pairings or carefully planned groupings of students according to your criteria, dictating where pupils sit can cause secondary behavioural issues.

However, on the whole, like a good sports coach, it helps to keep a handle on your team's formation and to have your cultural architects well spread across the room.

Experimentation is key here, as all good coaches know. The tactical placing of 'players' does not always produce the right result, but if you remain flexible and sensitive to feedback you can create the right result over time.

Getting it right – calibrated warnings and sanctions

Calibration is a useful NLP tool. It describes the measurement of something against a recognised standard. If, for example, a pupil is agitated, a teacher with sensory acuity can recognise this unusual state and alter their behaviour accordingly, creating rapport with the student, before leading them back to close concentration on their work.

They can also be sensitive to the application of both warnings and sanctions with individual students and, crucially, pace those students before leading them towards the discipline process.

Typically, cultural architects will receive so many warnings and sanctions from different teachers in an average week that they become meaningless. Teachers with good rapport skills learn how to endow those sanctions with meaning and make them part of the relationship with that individual, who, under normal circumstances, won't want to jeopardise that relationship by getting into conflict.

Calibration explained

> *'The pupil is always suggesting that he will withdraw his affection from the teacher, like the child from his parent, unless a demand is dropped. If your demand is legitimate and for the pupil's good, don't be tempted to abandon it.'* **Michael Marland**

There are certain students who simply need more warnings and who take up more time than others in the struggle to get them onside. Sanctioning early can be counterproductive with these pupils. However, a teacher who is prepared to be patient will often be rewarded, as long as they remain assertive and follow through on warnings.

A pupil may behave well if they know that you will allow them some leeway but there will always be occasions where they test your resolve or, as Marland noted, threaten to 'withdraw affection' or co-operation. It is for this reason that it is vital to remain assertive, even whilst maintaining rapport.

When you can sanction a cultural architect and then re-integrate them into your classes, you will be well on the way to balancing the triad of skills discussed in this book.

Calibration examples

Flexibility in your language and gestures is key to calibrating your responses.
The result is that you allow those pupils who require more thinking or take-up time to respond in the way that you ultimately want. Here are a few examples:

- Rhetorical questions – *'Brent, do you need a warning?'* (Said in a non-combative tone that alerts Brent to the need to rein in his behaviour before he goes too far.)
- Direct instructions – *'Anya, you need to concentrate on finishing this section now.'*
- Redirective questions – *'How's it going? Do you need me to check how you're doing so far?'*
- Adding consequences to particular behaviours with increasing severity, but reminding pupils that they have some choice in the matter: *'Frankie, if you... ... you'll be choosing to move/ see me after the lesson/ leave the room.'*
- Empathising choice: *'If that's what you've chosen ....I'll have to...'* (Shows that the consequence is the result of a behaviour choice.)
- Physical cues: breaking eye contact and turning away, indicating that you expect compliance; stopping what you are saying and giving a long stare or raised eyebrows to indicate that you are unhappy or surprised at being interrupted; thumbs up and a smile to show approval, clapping hands, or some other pre-arranged signal to gain attention, etc

Being a role model

> 'If there is anything that we wish to change in the child, we should first examine it and see whether it is not something that could better be changed in ourselves. Children are educated by what the grown-up is and not by his talk.' **Carl Jung**

Children relate to you according to how they feel about you. They know if you care or not; they know how you feel about your job, your subject and your profession. You are leaking this information all the time and your students pick up on it. A great teacher inspires pupils to learn.

It's time to do an audit of yourself as a caring, passionate teacher. Put yourself in your students' shoes and answer the following questions about the kind of role model you are:

- How much does this teacher care about me and my progress? What do they do to let me know?
- How much does this teacher care about whether I understand the lesson or not. How do I know?
- Does this teacher like me? What do they do to show me?
- Does this teacher like their subject and like teaching it to me? How do I know?
- Do they like my class? Does my class like them?

High standards – self-fulfilling prophecies

> *'When we expect certain behaviors of others, we are likely to act in ways that make the expected behavior more likely to occur.'* **(Rosenthal and Babad, 1985)**

Here's what American psychologist and professor of Human Development at Cornell University, Bob Sternberg has to say about his school years:

> *'My teachers thought I was a big dope. When I grew up we did group IQ tests every year or two (which I failed). Since my teachers thought I was stupid, I thought I was stupid and since I thought I was stupid, I did stupid work and they were happy that I did stupid work, because I was meeting their expectation; and I was happy that they were happy and everyone was pretty happy.*
>
> *It wasn't until I was in 4th grade that I had a teacher, Mrs Alexa, who thought that there was something more to a student than a test score and she expected more from me and I gave her more...so I became a good student; so I defeated that self-fulfilling prophecy but many students don't have a teacher like Mrs Alexa and they become victims of that self-fulfilling prophecy.'* **Bob Sternberg**

High standards – self-fulfilling prophecies

Mrs Alexa got results by using what Rosenthal and Jacobsen (1968)* described as the Pygmalion Effect. They found that teacher expectations influence student performance. It works both ways:

Positive expectations influence performance positively, and negative expectations influence performance negatively.

*Rosenthal, R, and Jacobsen L. *Pygmalion in the classroom: teacher expectation and pupils' intellectual development*. New York: Holt, Rinehart and Winston, 1968.

High standards – embracing growth mindset

Carol Dweck's work on Growth Mindset has been hugely influential in shaping 21st century teaching. Dweck's work distinguishes between what she calls 'fixed' and 'growth' mindsets and is explored in a school context in the *Growth Mindset Pocketbook*.

The key point is that teachers who believe that intelligence is fixed may unconsciously be discounting various pupils whose data 'proves' that they 'will not succeed' academically. If your beliefs are picked up by those pupils, then their fixed mindset is simply reinforced, leading to even lower self-confidence and motivation.

High standards – embracing growth mindset

Fixed Mindset	Growth Mindset
Intelligence is fixed: you are 'good' at something or not	Intelligence is fluid. You can improve as a result of concentrated effort
Praise awarded for 'intelligence' and test scores	Praise awarded for effort
Tell me the answer: I just want to get it right	Let's discuss how we learn best and enjoy the process of trial and error in problem solving
I only want to do what I am good at. / This is too hard	I want to challenge myself to develop. I don't mind making mistakes

High standards – how you convey them

John, a secondary school science teacher, tells each class at the beginning of the year that he will demand their best work in his lessons. He establishes high standards and a growth mindset as part of his persona.

> *'I promise them that I will come to each lesson and give them everything I have because I am a perfectionist and I will be exhausted at the end of the lesson, so I expect them to put in as much effort as I do. I tell them not to coast in years 7, 8 and 9, but to make the most of each lesson with me....basically I demand that they respect themselves as learners; that's a big thing with me.'*

Some ways to communicate your high standards:

- Regular marking and feedback on their work
- Well prepared and presented lessons
- Public praise for effort and hard work
- Scaffolding and differentiating work
- Sharing success
- A clearly explained and consistently applied system of rewards and sanctions

It won't come as a surprise that John's classes live up to his expectations.

Introduction

 Status

 Assertiveness

 Rapport

 Three Circles of Energy

 Only Connect

 Voice, Costume, Space

Voice, Costume, Space

What's in your toolbox

So far I have described how teachers can balance a triad of skills (status, assertiveness and rapport) to create a winning teacher persona. We've also looked at how great teachers use their understanding of energy to create an ordered, well-managed environment. These teachers are able to draw their pupils into a shared second circle of energy, where real learning can take place. We've seen also how tools and techniques from NLP and psychology have a place in helping to develop our persona and presence.

Finally, we need to explore which aspects of acting, performance and stagecraft belong in a teacher's toolbox:

- How can an awareness of voice production affect your presence?
- Does what you wear have an impact on your students?
- Are you able to maximise your understanding of space, particularly when teaching outside of a traditional classroom?
- How can you use aspects of actor training to create a believable and powerful persona?
- What can be learnt from teachers who teach Drama and Theatre in unconventional spaces?

Breathing and voice

Think about your breathing and your voice. Become aware of your breathing right now as you are reading this page, and simply focus on keeping your back straight and your head still. What do you notice?

- Do you notice your stomach starting to expand and fill with air?
- Do you notice your breath becoming slightly deeper?
- Do you notice a subtle shift in your thoughts and emotions?

Now try something else. Maybe wait until you are alone for this one as it involves making some sound! Make sure you're in the 'head still and back straight' position (standing or sitting is fine). Take a minute and focus on allowing the air to come in through your nose and out through your mouth. Once this has become comfortable, allow some sound to come out of your mouth on your 'out breath', an *'aaahhh'* sound. Notice the pitch, tone and register.

Now go back to your original position and notice what happens to your breathing. The likelihood is that it will become rather more shallow. You may no longer be able to fill your stomach and if you try to make exactly the same sound, it may come out sounding different.

Breathing and voice

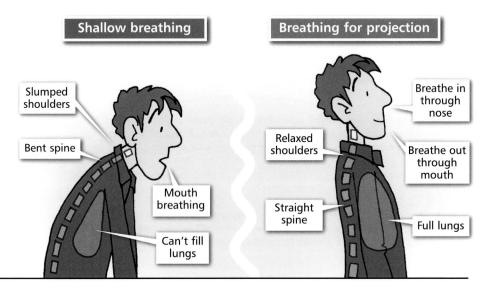

Shallow breathing

- Slumped shoulders
- Bent spine
- Mouth breathing
- Can't fill lungs

Breathing for projection

- Breathe in through nose
- Relaxed shoulders
- Breathe out through mouth
- Straight spine
- Full lungs

Voice training

What you have just experienced is voice training in a nutshell. Vocal skills are essential for actors, singers, public speakers or anyone who makes a living trying to fill an auditorium with the sound of their voice without ruining their voice.

But hold on.....don't you do that all day? Maybe not in an auditorium as such but you are certainly a public speaker.

What you experienced if you tried the previous exercise is what voice teachers would call your 'natural voice'. It tends to be deeper, more resonant and more powerful than our everyday voice. This is because it comes from a different place: the stomach rather than the chest and throat.

Breathing in this way allows actors and singers to project their voices and to create a deep, resonant and pleasing sound, which can express the full range of emotions. Shallow breathing on the other hand tends to produce a higher-pitched sound, with less power and emotional range.

Sing your natural voice

The natural voice, because it is fully connected to your breath, is the voice that singers and actors use to communicate powerful emotion in their music or words and you can do this too. Think back to communicating with your audience in second circle. Your natural voice is where you connect with others by investing more of yourself and your feelings through your words.

- Become aware of how you breathe in lessons
- When you are addressing the class, try to breathe deeply and notice how the sound changes
- Notice any new reactions from your pupils
- Try to use this voice whenever you need to correct or criticise students as it carries more authority and 'weight'

Voice and the 'Iron Lady'

The film *The King's Speech* gives an insight into how voice coaching and training was used in the 1920s to transform King George VI's ability to communicate to the nation. Many 21st century politicians with perceived 'image problems' have taken advice on voice production. Scottish politician Nicola Sturgeon has admitted that the actor Sean Connery gave her advice on voice production after her appearance and demeanour were ridiculed in the press. She learnt to create a more powerful presence by projecting her voice.

Possibly the most impressive vocal transformation was that made by Margaret Thatcher, who famously worked with a voice coach from the Royal National Theatre. The transformation was so successful that it has been studied by academics. Her 'before and after' performances show that she achieved a reduction in pitch of 46 Hz – almost half the average difference in pitch between male and female voices. The 'after' performance is a near perfect example of 'slower and lower' where you breathe from the diaphragm, develop a lower vocal range and become slower, more deliberate, and emphatic with your words.

Just watch the difference!
https://www.youtube.com/watch?v=28_0gXLKLbk

Voice and the 'Iron Lady'

There is more that we can learn from Thatcher's performance skills than simply tone and register. Her theatrical voice training quite possibly included aspects of the Stanislavsky System of actor training. Stanislavsky was director of the Moscow Art Theatre, from 1897 until the 1920's and was credited with developing the naturalistic acting style which became known in the USA as 'The Method'. It still forms the basis of much actor training in the world today.

In Thatcher's first interview clip, you will notice that as an untrained rookie politician, who has become the first female UK Prime Minister, she smiles when she says:

> *I know that I'm still only me and so do my family…. but I am very much aware of the responsibilities and a little bit apprehensive… who wouldn't be, when you think of the names that I follow.*

Everything about the words, the voice and the smile says: 'I'm new to this and I've not yet fully embraced this role so please be nice and give me time'. She could be a new teacher trying to ingratiate herself with a new class!

Voice and the 'Iron Lady'

Actors being trained in the Stanislavsky system, are taught that any line of script must have a purpose and that the actor's job is to uncover the specific purpose of each line by discovering its subtext. The question to ask is: 'What change do I want to produce in the other actor?' That specific change is referred to by actors as the intention or the objective of the character. In the 'after' clip, filmed towards the end of her career, Thatcher is powerfully defending her government's record against charges of social divisiveness.

*Let me answer that **very** deeply (pause)*
Objective: to correct (you have just offended me)
*I feel **very** strongly about it*
Objective: to warn (you've messed up; this is personal)
*The greatest divisions this nation has **ever** seen were the conflicts*
of trade unions towards the end of a Labour Government
Objective: to teach/ put you straight (My tenure has not been in the least divisive compared to my predecessors')

When actors play their objectives strongly and learn to pause and to emphasise certain words, the audience feels the emotional charge. As we will see on the next page, teachers can also learn how to use objectives to dramatically enhance the impact of their words.

Delivering your lines

A theatre director will often take a line of text and improvise with an actor in order to uncover its subtext. Only then will they put the text 'back on top' so that it sounds both purposeful and convincing. As a teacher you can experiment in the same way with certain pre-determined words and phrases. It is also worth experimenting with where you place the emphasis in the line, as placement can make all the difference.

Given Circumstances	Line / Emphasis	Objective	Subtext
Class questioning	This is a **higher** order question… you'll **all** be able to tackle it.	To inspire /encourage	We are aiming high and I believe in every one of you.
Class are slow to start	I see that **Amy** has opened her book.	To positively influence others	'Praise envy'. I'm not going to complain, just focus on what is going well.
One pupil is out of his seat	Brian, you **need** to sit down.	To instruct	I am a high status teacher whose instructions you need to follow.
Noise levels too high	This is **very** disappointing.	To refocus	I take your progress personally.

Costume – why it matters

It's all too easy to undermine your carefully developed high status persona and presence by what you could call 'poor costume choices'. This is why I want to explain how central the idea of costume is to anyone involved in the performance arts, and that includes teaching.

Before the New York inspired 'method acting' became fashionable in British film and theatre, our stages were populated by giants like Laurence Olivier, who would often find the costume before the internal truth of the character, such was their appreciation of external detail.

That generation of actors is legendary for attention to external detail. Anthony Quinn, when filming Lawrence of Arabia with Olivier, apparently spent hours perfecting his make-up and appearance for the character of the tribal leader he was playing. He arrived on set on the first day of filming in full costume and make-up. The director David Lean had no idea who this new 'extra' was but wanted to cast him for the role instead of Quinn!

It must have seemed obvious to these actors that costume not only communicates volumes to the audience but it also changes the way the actor feels about himself and the character.

The teacher's costume

'Pupils have certain expectations. The first of these is an only half-conscious feeling that if he cares about us, he'll care how he looks for us ...They are thrown by the slightly aggressive, uncertain choice of whatever is the way out vogue; they are depressed by the badly worn; and they are insulted by the torn and dirty.'
Michael Marland, *The Craft of the Classroom*

At the time, 1975, Marland was a working headteacher in a London school. Things have moved on considerably since the 70's but the way we dress inevitably makes an impression on our 21st century students. It's a point worth considering.

Power dressing?

> 'One of my colleagues was notorious for being a sloppy dresser, literally like he'd just rolled out of bed. He was also notorious for having badly behaved classes. Except for his 'suit days'. Occasionally he would dig out his black suit and report how, magically, the kids had all behaved well that day. It's so easy for men; just throw on a suit and tie and you're done.' **Mandy, English teacher**

Here are a few 'costume rules' derived from the ideas I have explored so far:

- What you wear affects the way you feel about yourself and how your audience relate to you
- Teachers who have a high status persona (and confidence) can afford to pay less attention to what they wear: we've all seen casually dressed teachers with great discipline
- Think about clothes as part of your persona and choose them accordingly: if you are creating a high status persona you may want to experiment with power dressing: it's called that for a reason!

School uniform

In the UK at least, most schools still insist that pupils 'dress up' for school.
Here are a few ideas to remember about uniform:

- Insisting on pupils wearing their uniform correctly is part of your teacher persona: deal with the small details and the bigger matters often take care of themselves
- If they are dressed smartly, they will expect you to be
- There will be an often unwritten 'dress code' amongst staff. Make your own decisions about whether you feel that it helps or hinders school discipline and don't be afraid to 'do different'

Spatial awareness

When I trained as a theatre director one of my first tasks was to understand the various implications of positioning actors on stage.

A simple example would be using a triangular grouping, with the character in focus upstage at the tip of the triangle and the two downstage actors looking towards that character. These groupings help to focus the audience's attention where it is needed.

Spatial awareness relates to the classroom in that although teachers no longer routinely use a rostrum to elevate them physically above their class, there is normally a recognised 'stage' and 'auditorium' in most classrooms.

Spatial awareness II

I stress the idea of stage and auditorium because your energy as a teacher changes in each of these areas. Like the actor on stage at the apex of a triangle, you are most visible when you are on stage, in the middle, at the front. You also have most power in terms of class focus and energy.

The minute you wander into the auditorium your energy becomes more diffuse. Pupils are less likely to listen and more likely to talk. You can experiment with these ideas as follows, imagining yourself as a theatre director:

- Try speaking to the class from different parts of the room and see which is most and least successful. In theory 'the front' of the room is where you are positioned at any given point, although speaking from different parts of the room may have different effects on your students. Check for responses (in terms of class noise and general concentration)
- Start to become aware of only giving (the most important) instructions when you are centre front and notice the subtle changes in your students
- Be aware that you can always coach, encourage and model success from any desk in the room: *'Let's just stop and listen to how John has approached this answer'*

Different spaces – the circle

Most teachers are used to fairly standard classrooms and will rarely, if ever, need to move outside the confines of 30 chairs, desks and a whiteboard. But what if your normal teaching space isn't like this? For the first 16 years of my career I worked mainly in a variety of non-classroom environments: large empty spaces such as school halls or dining halls and, if I was really lucky, drama studios.

You can be teaching in a massive hall but if your class is in a circle, then the learning space is that shared space in front of you. Learning to teach in a circle is in many ways more challenging than teaching in a regular classroom space because:

- Sitting as part of a circle is a more democratic experience than addressing a class sitting at tables in front of you. Good in principle, but less easy to manage in practice
- From a status point of view, you need to learn the fine balancing act of keeping your status high whilst encouraging students to speak from the sides and to perform in the centre of the circle
- The fact that pupils can see each other at all times can work for or against you. You have created a second circle shared space for them and this shared space has to be managed well

Different spaces – the power of the circle

Mastering the circle is about maximising its power as a performance space and not confusing it with a classroom. Anyone who speaks in the circle has everyone's full attention. Therefore, a discussion is very powerful, as each time you make a contribution you are effectively 'performing'. Of course the same rule applies to misbehaviour. Your job as 'circle manager' is to direct the group's focus at all times.

Maximise the potential of the space in front of you by using it for performing!

- Use volunteers to model skills or techniques
- Ask audience members for feedback (refer to them as an 'audience' to endow them with a shared identity)
- Have group discussions

What you might notice is that you end up teaching highly interactive, multi-sensory, exciting lessons that pupils look forward to. Teach in a space like this for a few weeks and you might never want to return to a classroom with desks in rows.

Different spaces – working in a circle

When planning lessons in a large space, use a circle of chairs as a start and end point of your lessons. Build in time for interactivity, but in groups with a common purpose and a deadline. Here's how I ran a successful lesson on assertiveness for a group of 30 x 12 year olds in a school hall:

- Circle time at the start to focus pupils and introduce topic
- Everyone fills in a child-friendly multiple choice assertiveness questionnaire
- Volunteers role play assertive, passive and aggressive behaviour in a given scenario, eg being bullied at school
- Class discuss pros and cons of each type of behaviour (how best to beat bullies)
- Group work in fours; choose one scenario from worksheet and give examples of the three reactions. Rehearsal to be monitored by teacher with strict time limit and countdown as minutes elapse
- Back to (semi) circle for seven two-minute performances from each group
- Evaluation and feedback

Different spaces – mastering the circle

It's easy to fail at large space teaching if you don't master the potential of a circle 'for good or evil' and if you struggle to manage groups in a large space.

Group work in a role play situation is full of potential pitfalls and a skilled teacher will learn how to finely balance their status and set the tone between 'controlled fun' and 'work'.

PROBLEMS	SOLUTIONS
Pupils don't stay in one space	Allocate each group a space to work and stay in. Establish 'space invading' as misbehaviour.
Pupils won't work together	Allow them to choose groups/ reserve right to move people.
Pupils don't do the work	Try directing their efforts/ warn and sanction as necessary.
Pupils don't work to time	Regular countdowns, regular monitoring of problem groups.
Noise level too high	Establish a 'my hand up = silence' rule at the outset. Use it to manage noise level. Keep rehearsal time to a minimum.

Speaking to the class – getting their attention

Any live performance you see will be preceded by various rituals which prompt the audience to focus on the performer, whether it is the lights going down in a cinema or theatre, or an MC introducing a comic.

A teacher does not have this luxury, despite needing to present a number of small 'performances' each lesson. There is no MC and there are no house lights so you need to establish your own signal to the audience to ensure that your performance does not fall on deaf ears.

The golden rule is not to speak unless there is silence and all eyes are on you. Here are some guidelines:

- Countdowns work well. Timed activities during lessons help to train pupils to respond to these
- Take up your position. Be visible, silent, still and calm; model what you want the class to achieve
- Use names calmly for those not focused

- Be prepared to warn and sanction compulsive talkers (silence is golden and must be won)
- Once won you can insist on silent working at any point if concentration is lost (most useful!)

Speaking to the class – adjusting your language

Working in Special Education gave me a unique insight into what teachers did that worked in the classroom. I was able to get a pupil's eye view of lessons and often hear moment-to-moment pupil feedback on a teacher's performance. One incident stays in my mind. A girl I was working with, who had moderate learning difficulties and speech and language impairment, used to regularly complain about one teacher in particular. This woman's crime was quite simply:

> She talks too posh!

What she meant was that the teacher's language was too complex for her to understand. My student was teaching me one of the pre-suppositions of NLP: 'the meaning of your communication is the response you get'. The type of language that I used as a teacher changed quite dramatically whilst working with these children. I often found myself 'translating' what the teacher had said.

The reality for these pupils was simple: most teachers talked way too much and assumed they were being understood when often their language – vocabulary, sentence structure, word order, etc – was inaccessible.

Speaking to the class – don't talk too much!

Special Education also taught me something very useful about teaching in general and that is that what's good for Special Needs pupils is usually good for all pupils. Often, the strategies you would use to scaffold/ differentiate a lesson here represent good practice generally.

At the point of writing, 'teacher talk' has become something of an issue in British education, with teachers being asked to limit their talk so that the ratio of pupil-to-teacher-led activities is around 70:30. I am wary of 'ratios' such as this, but the emphasis on 'designing learning experiences' has much to recommend it. Here are a few pointers:

- Be aware that many pupils cannot access the information via just one learning style (auditory)
- Have as many visual aids as possible to reinforce learning (on the board, on screen, in handouts)
- Pupils enjoy feeling part of a class and can enjoy being taught (not lectured to) from the front
- Put the main idea at the start of your sentence
- Simplify your language (or give two versions, one of which is simplified) and ask yourself if you are being as brief and clear as possible

Last words

I hope that in this Pocketbook I have been able to introduce you to ideas and concepts that are new to you, or which you have not seen combined or applied in this way before. If the idea of classroom presence has seemed nebulous or elusive, or if you have been looking for different ways of establishing yourself with particular classes, I hope you have found guidance and inspiration here.

I've managed to remain in teaching for over twenty years, partly because I don't see mastering the craft of teaching as markedly different from learning any other skill. Modelling excellence in one area, will often bring up universal principles. The experience of teachers is really not that different to the experience of performers, business people and sportsmen and women – and my approach has always been to learn from these groups, importing their expertise, to inform my own professional development.

I do hope that you will try out some of the ideas in the book and send me your thoughts, feedback and experiences. I am continually refining and improving my classroom practice and would love to keep learning from you. You can contact me at: robsalter51@gmail.com

Good Luck!

Recommended reading

The Craft of the Classroom
by Michael Marland. Heinemann, 1975

Dumbing Us Down: The Hidden Curriculum of Compulsory Schooling
by John Taylor Gatto. New Society Publishers, 2002

Effective Classroom Communication Pocketbook
by Richard Churches. Teachers' Pocketbooks, 2010

Impro – Improvisation and the Theatre
by Keith Johnstone. Eyre Methuen, 1981

Mindset: The New Psychology of Success
by Carol Dweck. Ballantine, 2008

NLP for Teachers
by Richard Churches and Roger Terry. Crown House, 2007

Presence: How to Use Positive Energy for Success in Every Situation
by Patsy Rodenburg. Penguin, 2009

To Sell is Human: The Surprising Truth about Persuading, Convincing and Influencing Others
by Daniel H. Pink. Canongate Books, 2014

About the author

Rob Salter

Rob graduated in French from The University of East Anglia and has an MA in Theatre Directing from Hull University. He worked as a freelance theatre director in London in the early 1990's and co-ran St. Raph's Children's Theatre. He has been a member of the Royal Court Theatre's Adult Writers' Group and has had rehearsed readings of a number of his plays.

It was during a sixteen-year period of teaching Drama in London schools that Rob first began to include performance techniques in his mentoring of student teachers. He became a Teaching and Learning Coach whilst working as a Special Needs Teacher. His popular website www.teaching-strategies-for-classroom-discipline.com, is a free online resource for teachers, on behaviour management, differentiation and special education issues. It carries details of his self-published *Behaviour Blueprint* (2011)

Rob now runs Meta Consulting – an educational consultancy specialising in metacognitive approaches to teaching and learning – and delivers individual teacher coaching via video call. He is currently working with a number of London secondary schools as a virtual coach, and is helping them to set up in-house coaching programmes.

Rob can be contacted at robsalter51@gmail.com

Order Form

Your details

Name _____

Position _____

School _____

Address _____

_____

_____

Telephone _____

Fax _____

E-mail _____

VAT No. (EC only) _____

Your Order Ref _____

Please send me:

No. copies

Classroom Presence _____ Pocketbook [ ]

_____ Pocketbook [ ]

_____ Pocketbook [ ]

_____ Pocketbook [ ]

Order by Post
Teachers' Pocketbooks
Laurel House, Station Approach
Alresford, Hants. SO24 9JH UK

Order by Phone, Fax or Internet
Telephone: +44 (0)1962 735573
Facsimile: +44 (0)1962 733637
Email: sales@teacherspocketbooks.co.uk
Web: www.teacherspocketbooks.co.uk

Customers in USA should contact:
2427 Bond Street, University Park, IL 60466
Tel: 866 620 6944 Facsimile: 708 534 7803
Email: mp.orders@ware-pak.com
Web: www.Teacherspocketbooks.com

Pocketbooks – available in both paperback and digital formats

Teachers' Titles		Selected Management Titles
Accelerated Learning	Form Tutor's	Appraisals
Anger & Conflict Management	Gifted & Talented	Assertiveness
Asperger Syndrome	Growth Mindset	Confidence
Assessment & Learning	Handwriting	Delegation
Behaviour Management	Head of Department's	Emotional Intelligence
Boys, Girls & Learning	Independent Learning	Energy & Well-being
Challenging Behaviours	Learning & the Brain	Feedback
Classroom Presence	Learning to Learn	Icebreakers
Coaching & Reflecting	Lesson Observation	Impact & Presence
Collaborative Learning	Literacy Across the Curriculum	Influencing
Creative Teaching	Managing Workload	Leadership
Differentiation	Outstanding Lessons	Managing Change
Drama for Learning	P4C	Meetings
Dyscalculia	Primary Teacher's	Memory
Dyslexia	Questioning Technique	Mentoring
Dyspraxia/DCD	Raising Achievement	NLP
EAL	Restorative Justice	Openers & Closers
Eating Disorders	Speech, Language & Communication	Performance Management
Effective Classroom Communication	Teaching Assistant's	Personal Success
Emotional Literacy	Teaching Thinking	Presentations
		Resolving Conflict
		Succeeding at Interviews
		Stress
		Tackling Difficult Conversations
		Teamworking
		Time Management
		Trainer's
		Vocal Skills
		Workplace Politics

www.teacherspocketbooks.co.uk